W9-AAX-625

Art Smart

How to Draw Insects

Christine Smith

For a free color catalog describing Gareth Stevens Publishing's list of high-quality books and multimedia programs, call 1-800-542-2595 (USA) or 1-800-461-9120 (Canada). Gareth Stevens Publishing's Fax: (414) 225-0377.

Library of Congress Cataloging-in-Publication Data available upon request from the publisher. Fax: (414) 225-0377 for the attention of the Publishing Records Department.

ISBN 0-8368-1710-9

First published in North America in 1997 by
Gareth Stevens Publishing
1555 North RiverCenter Drive, Suite 201
Milwaukee, Wisconsin, 53212, USA

Original © 1996 by Regency House Publishing Limited (Troddy Books Imprint), The Grange, Grange Yard, London, England, SE1 3AG. Text and illustrations by Christine Smith. Additional end matter © 1997 by Gareth Stevens, Inc.

Printed in the United States of America

2 3 4 5 6 7 8 9 01 00 99

Gareth Stevens Publishing
MILWAUKEE

Materials

Drawing pencils have letters printed on them to show the firmness of the lead. Pencils with an *H* have very hard lead. Pencils with an *HB* have medium lead. Pencils with a *B* have soft lead. Use an *HB* pencil to draw the outlines in this book. Then use a *B* pencil to complete the drawings.

This type of pencil sharpener works well because it keeps the shavings inside a container.

Once you have drawn the outlines on a piece of paper, place a thinner sheet of paper over them. Then make a clean, finished drawing, leaving out any unnecessary lines.

Use a soft eraser to make any changes you might want. Color your drawings with felt-tip pens, watercolors, crayons, or colored pencils.

Shapes

Before you begin drawing, practice the shapes above. Draw them over and over again. All the drawings in this book are based on these simple shapes.

Color

Mixing colors is fun whether you are using colored pencils or paints. Mix red and yellow to make orange. Mix blue and yellow to make green. Red and blue make purple.

3

Butterflies and moths have beautiful patterns on their wings. On each butterfly or moth, the pattern is the same on both of its wings. To make sure the patterns you draw are identical, fold your sheet of paper in half and make a strong crease. Open the paper, and draw one half of the butterfly or moth, like this.

Then fold the paper back again and rub the back of the drawing with the rounded part of a spoon. Open the paper, and you will see the pattern repeated on the other side of the crease. Trace over the lines to make them darker.

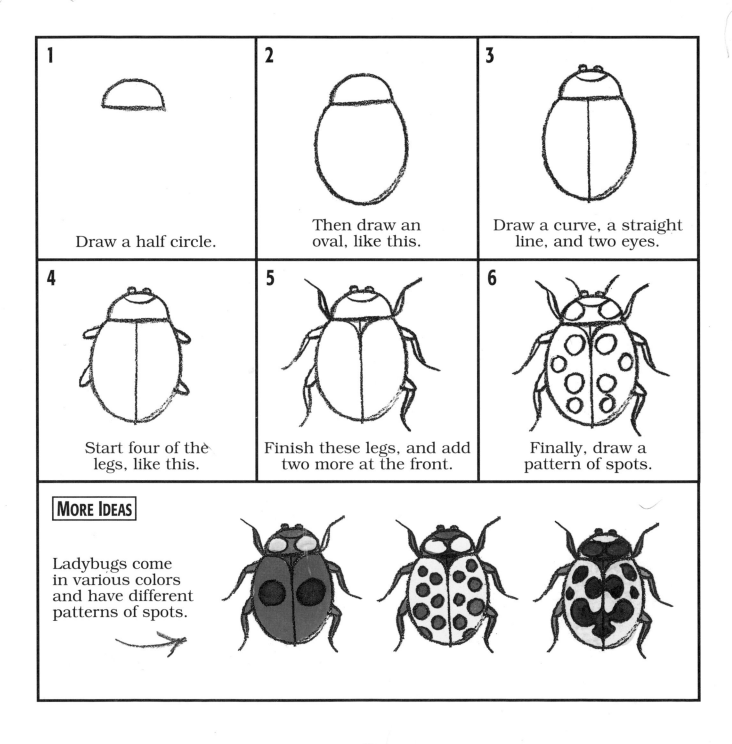

1 Draw a half circle.

2 Then draw an oval, like this.

3 Draw a curve, a straight line, and two eyes.

4 Start four of the legs, like this.

5 Finish these legs, and add two more at the front.

6 Finally, draw a pattern of spots.

MORE IDEAS

Ladybugs come in various colors and have different patterns of spots.

6

Ladybug

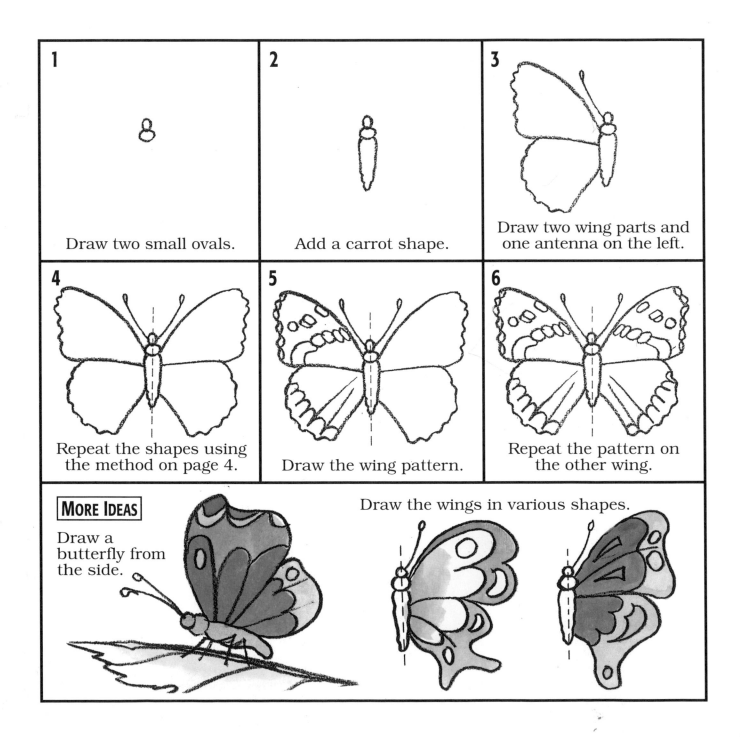

1
Draw two small ovals.

2
Add a carrot shape.

3
Draw two wing parts and one antenna on the left.

4
Repeat the shapes using the method on page 4.

5
Draw the wing pattern.

6
Repeat the pattern on the other wing.

MORE IDEAS

Draw a butterfly from the side.

Draw the wings in various shapes.

Butterfly

1

Draw an oval with a small one on top.

2

Draw a larger oval, like this.

3

Draw wings on each side.

4

Add the eyes and antennae.

5

Draw the legs.

6

Add the stripes and other finishing touches.

MORE IDEAS

Draw a pattern on the wings.

Draw the bee with its wings folded.

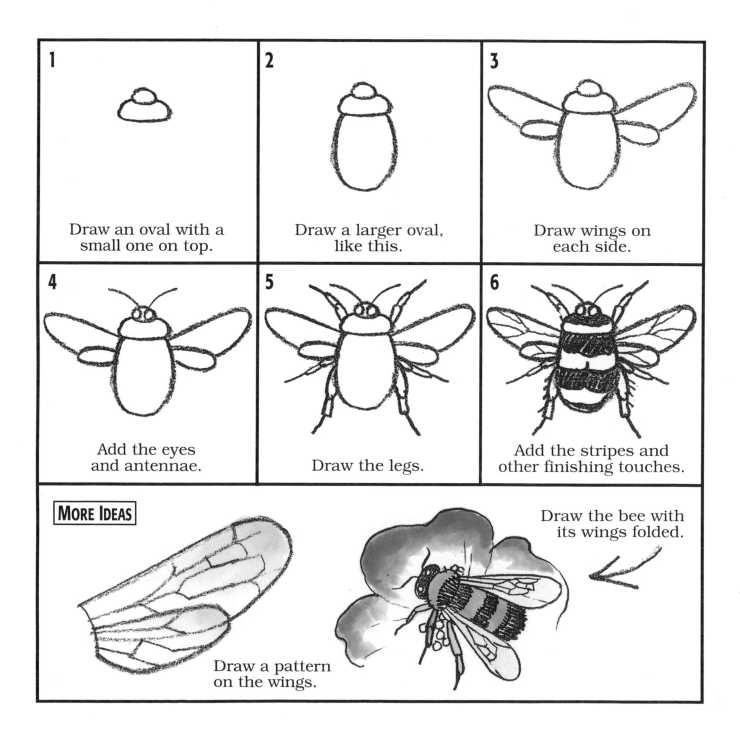

Bumblebee

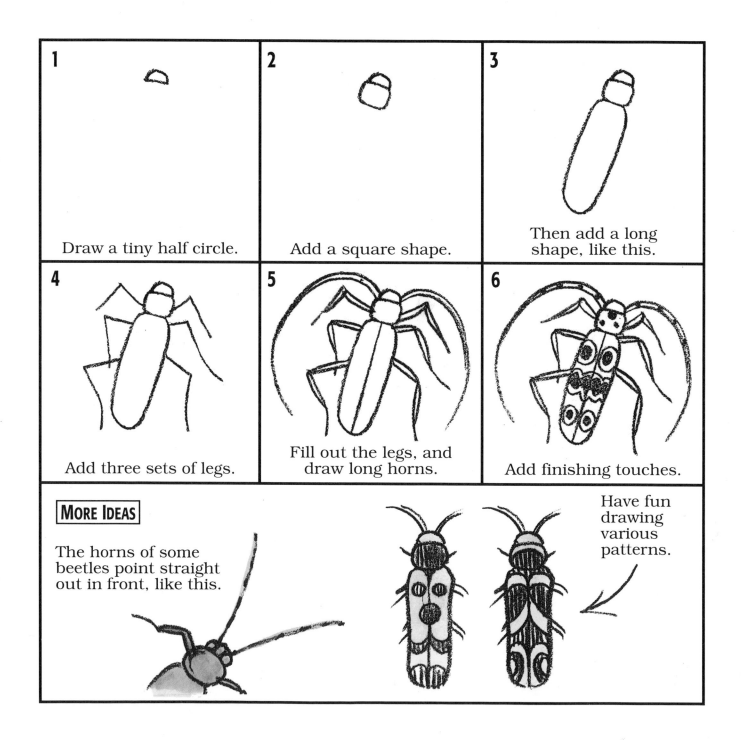

1 Draw a tiny half circle.

2 Add a square shape.

3 Then add a long shape, like this.

4 Add three sets of legs.

5 Fill out the legs, and draw long horns.

6 Add finishing touches.

MORE IDEAS

The horns of some beetles point straight out in front, like this.

Have fun drawing various patterns.

12

Longhorn beetle

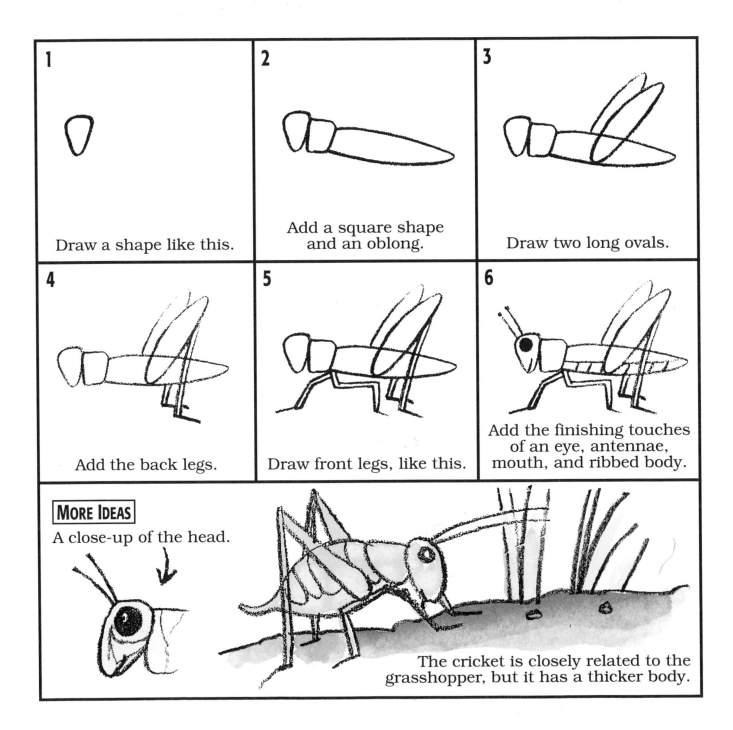

1 Draw a shape like this.

2 Add a square shape and an oblong.

3 Draw two long ovals.

4 Add the back legs.

5 Draw front legs, like this.

6 Add the finishing touches of an eye, antennae, mouth, and ribbed body.

MORE IDEAS

A close-up of the head.

The cricket is closely related to the grasshopper, but it has a thicker body.

14

Grasshopper

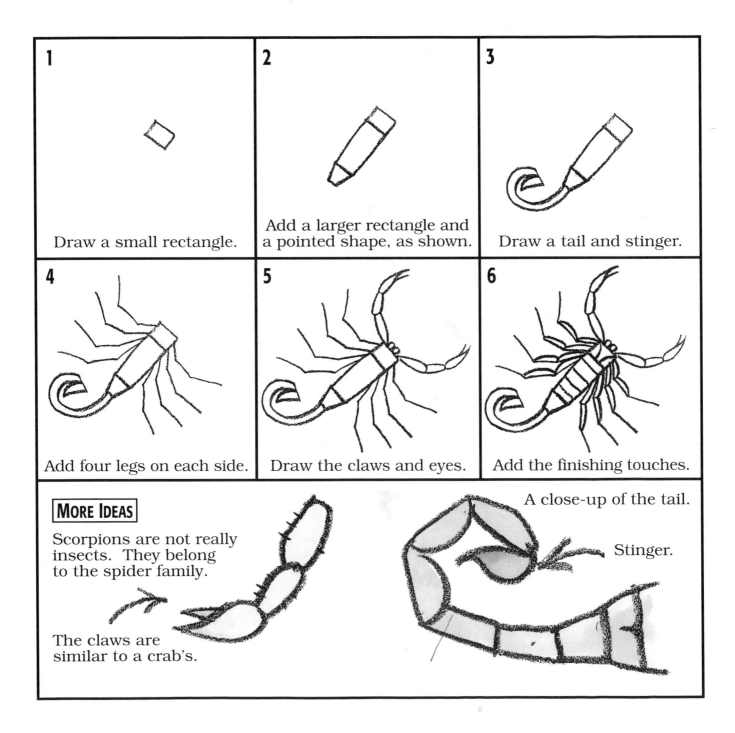

1
Draw a small rectangle.

2
Add a larger rectangle and a pointed shape, as shown.

3
Draw a tail and stinger.

4
Add four legs on each side.

5
Draw the claws and eyes.

6
Add the finishing touches.

MORE IDEAS

Scorpions are not really insects. They belong to the spider family.

The claws are similar to a crab's.

A close-up of the tail.

Stinger.

Scorpion

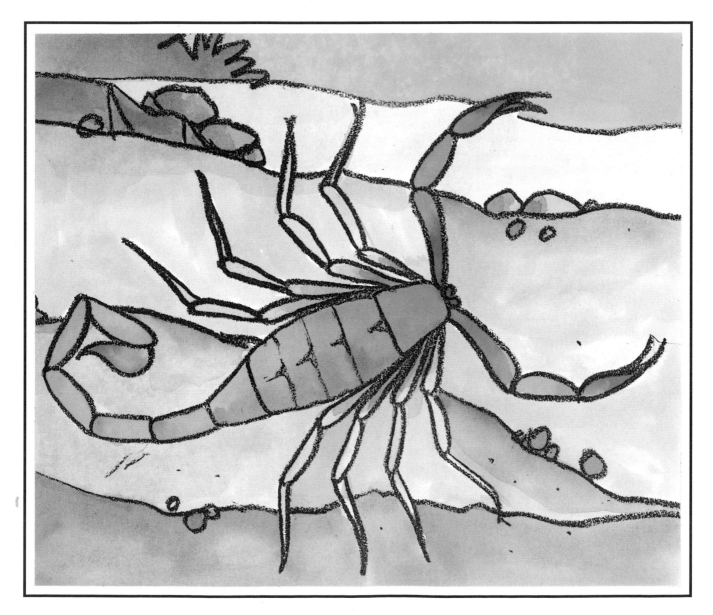

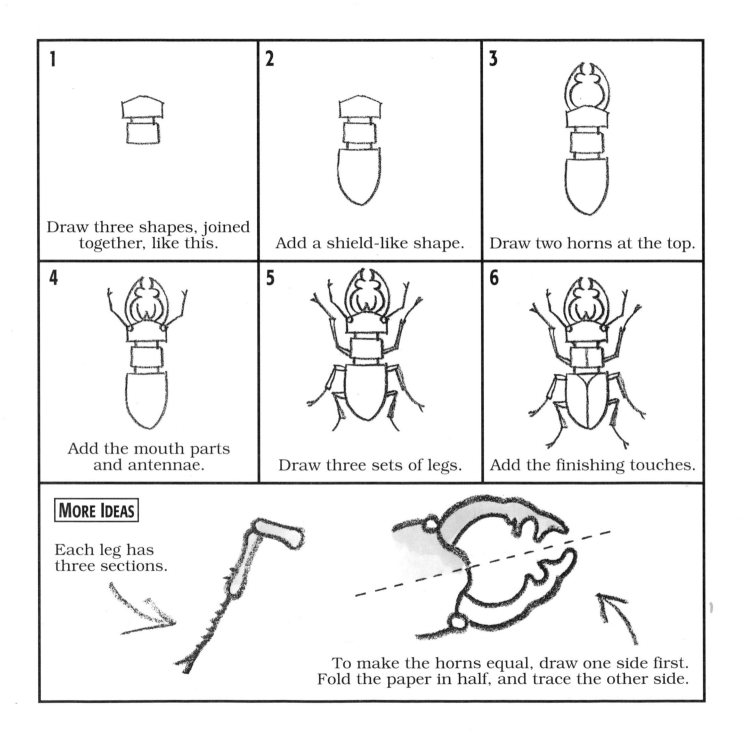

1
Draw three shapes, joined together, like this.

2
Add a shield-like shape.

3
Draw two horns at the top.

4
Add the mouth parts and antennae.

5
Draw three sets of legs.

6
Add the finishing touches.

MORE IDEAS

Each leg has three sections.

To make the horns equal, draw one side first. Fold the paper in half, and trace the other side.

Stag beetle

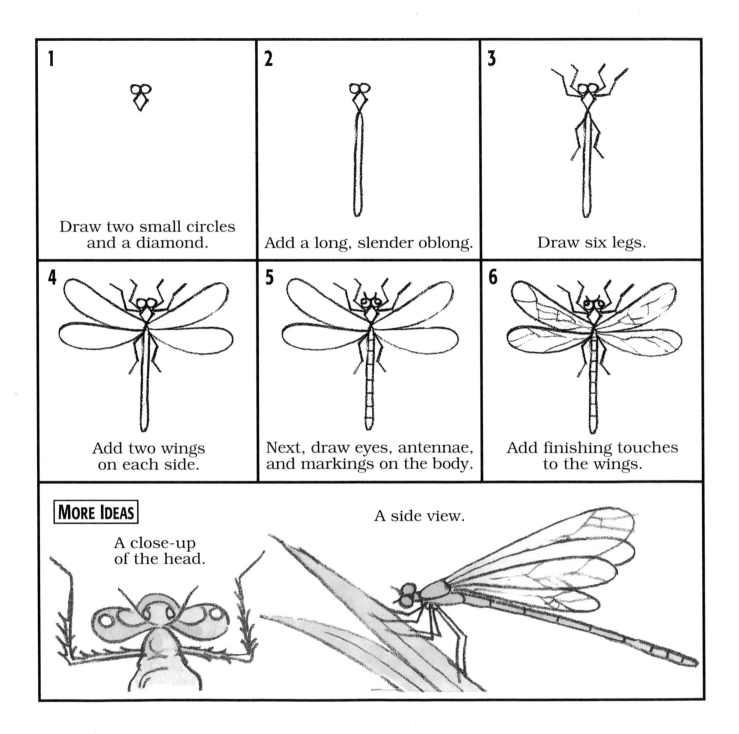

1 Draw two small circles and a diamond.

2 Add a long, slender oblong.

3 Draw six legs.

4 Add two wings on each side.

5 Next, draw eyes, antennae, and markings on the body.

6 Add finishing touches to the wings.

MORE IDEAS

A close-up of the head.

A side view.

20

Damselfly

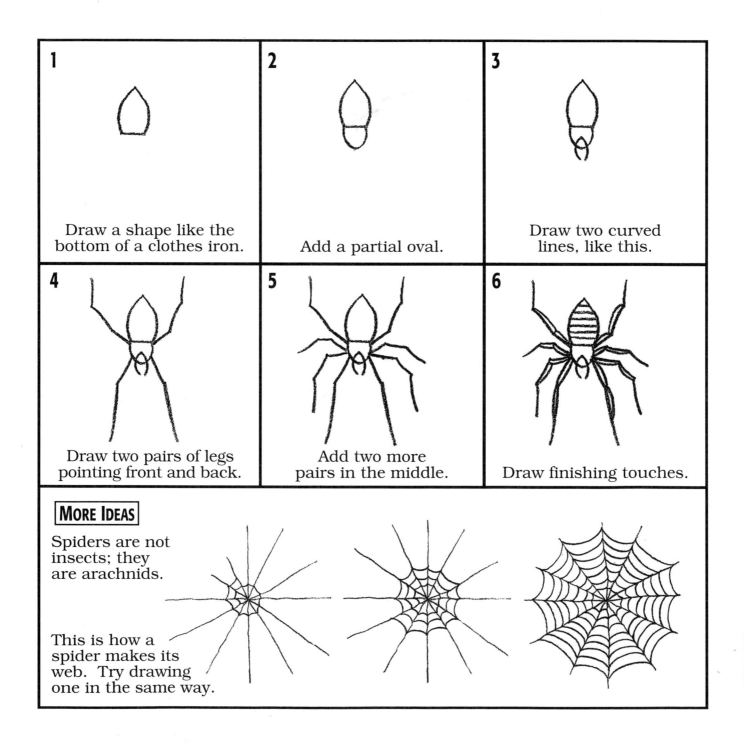

1

Draw a shape like the bottom of a clothes iron.

2

Add a partial oval.

3

Draw two curved lines, like this.

4

Draw two pairs of legs pointing front and back.

5

Add two more pairs in the middle.

6

Draw finishing touches.

MORE IDEAS

Spiders are not insects; they are arachnids.

This is how a spider makes its web. Try drawing one in the same way.

Spider

More Books to Read

Draw, Model, and Paint (series). (Gareth Stevens)
Flying Insects. Patricia Lantier-Sampon (Gareth Stevens)
How to Draw Creepy Creatures. Cindy Reisenauer (Kidsbooks)
I Can Draw Bugs. (W. Foster Publishing)
Ladybug. Emery Bernhard (Holiday)
The New Creepy Crawly Collection (series). (Gareth Stevens)
A Picture Book of Insects. Joanne Mattern (Troll Communications)
Worldwide Crafts (series). Deshpande/MacLeod-Brudenell (Gareth Stevens)

Videos

Basic Shapes, I and II. (Agency for Instructional Technology)
Discovering Form in Art. (Phoenix/BFA Films and Video)
The Insect Challenge. (Pyramid Film and Video)
Nature Drawings. (Roland Collection)
Super Bugs. (Agency for Instructional Technology)

Web Sites

http://www.go-interface.com/fridgeartz
http://finalfront.com/kids/art/art.htm

Index